Goats

Beverley Randell and Clive Harper

Contents

Billy goats, nanny goats and kids	2
Young kids	4
Goats on farms	6
All sorts of goats	8
Food for goats	10
Caring for goats	12
A long time ago	14
Goats climb anywhere	16

Billy goats, nanny goats and kids

Male goats are called billy goats.
Female goats are called nanny goats.
Baby goats are called kids.
Nanny goats can have kids when they are only one year old.

All goats butt with their heads. They butt other goats (and they butt people).

Most billy goats have beards and horns. Some billy goats have big horns that go up.

Some billy goats have big horns that go out sideways.

What are baby goats called?

Young kids

Most nanny goats
have two or three kids at a time.
If they have twin kids in the spring,
they can have twin kids again
in the autumn.

Baby goats are called kids.

A wild nanny goat
will hide her newborn kids
by a bush, or in the grass.
She will go away to feed,
but she will come back
to give milk to her kids.

Soon the kids
are ready to
run and skip,
climb and jump,
push and butt.
Kids play like children.
That's why children are called kids.

Can nanny goats have three kids at a time?

Goats on farms

Some farmers keep goats because they can shear them. When long-haired goats are shorn, their hair can be made into clothes and rugs.

Soft mohair rugs are made from goat hair.

Yes. Nanny goats can have three kids at a time.

Some nanny goats are kept
on farms because
they can be milked, like cows.
Some people cannot drink cows' milk
because it makes them sick,
but they can drink goats' milk.

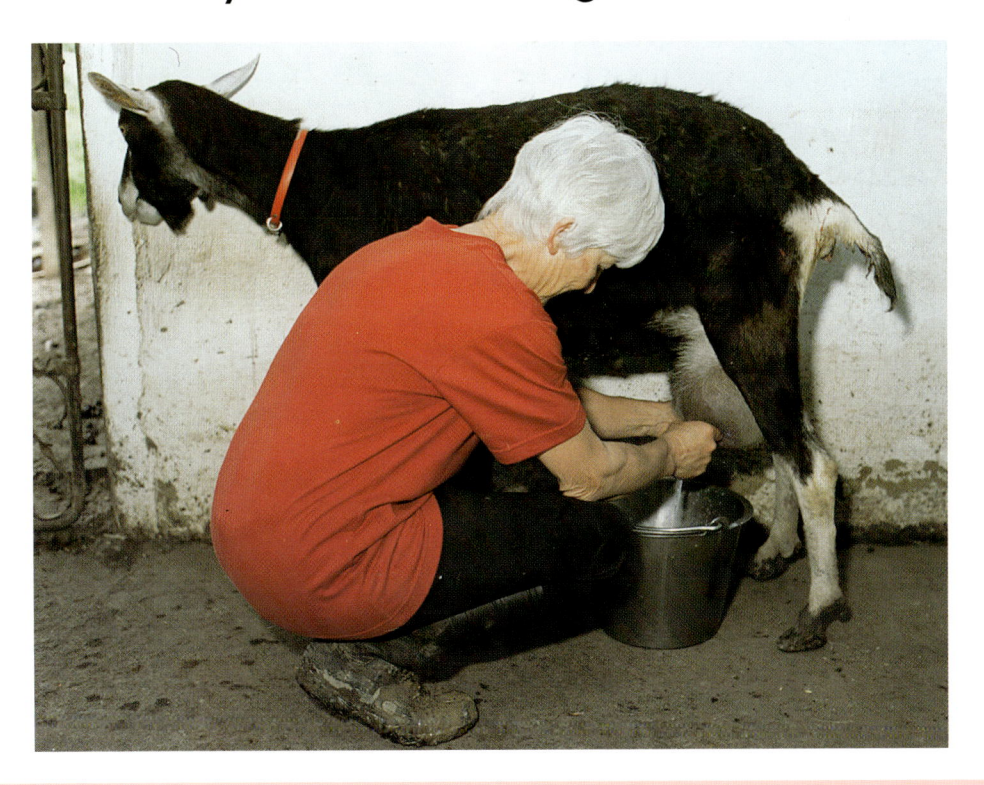

What can goats' hair be made into?

All sorts of goats

Goats can be
long-haired or short-haired.

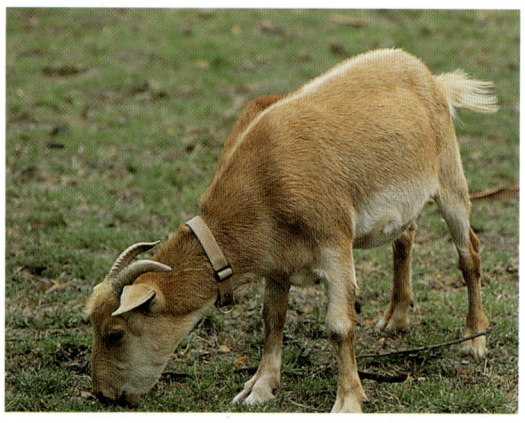

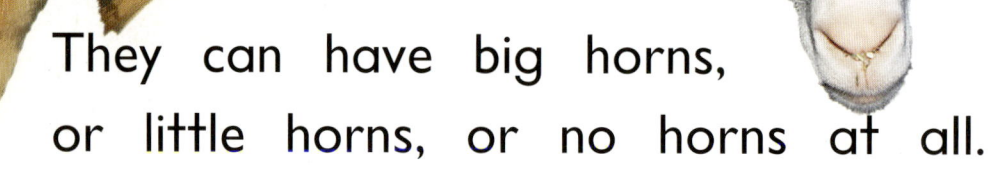

They can have big horns,
or little horns, or no horns at all.

Goats' hair can be made
into clothes and rugs.

Goats can be white, brown or black, or two or three colours.

They can be wild and dangerous, or tame and gentle like these ones.

Do all goats have horns?

Food for goats

Hungry goats will eat anything! Some farm goats are kept because they eat weeds.

Not all goats have horns.

Goats will eat grass, too,
but they love
eating leaves
and bark
from trees.
Goats can kill
young trees.
Sometimes they
even climb trees.

Goats eat fruit and vegetables
and grain and hay.
Goats chew the cud, as cattle do.
Sometimes they will eat paper.
Or old socks!

Why do goats climb trees?

Caring for goats

Goats that are milked must be kept very clean, and they need to be well fed.

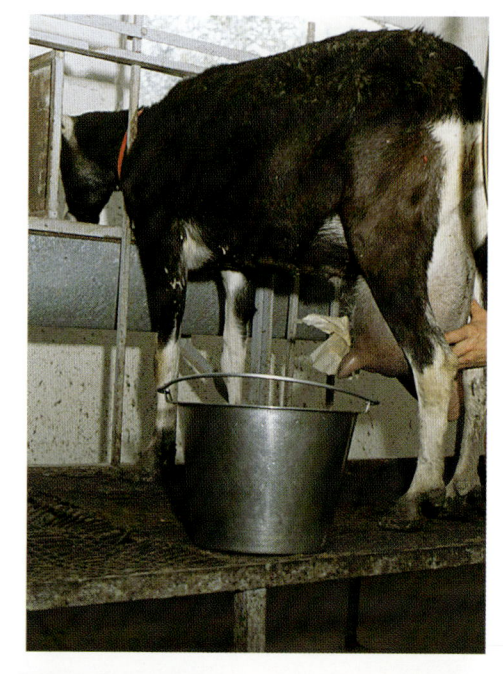

Vets know what to do when a goat is sick.

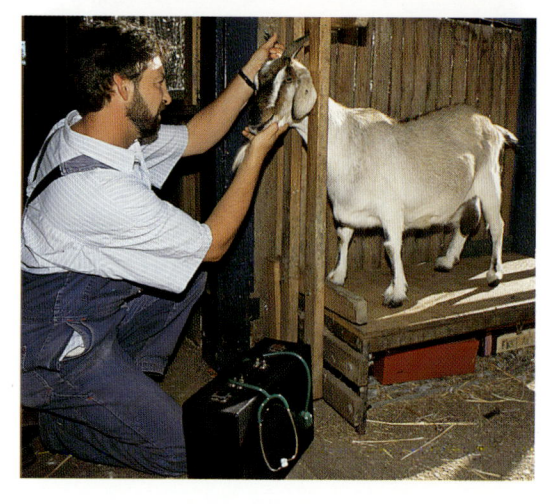

Goats climb trees to eat the leaves, and sometimes the fruit.

Goats are very good
at jumping over fences,
so farmers have to think
of ways to keep them in.
Sometimes goats are tied up.

Why are goats sometimes tied up?

A long time ago

A long time ago,
all goats were wild.
Many goats lived
in high rocky places
in Europe and Asia.
Wild goats still live there.

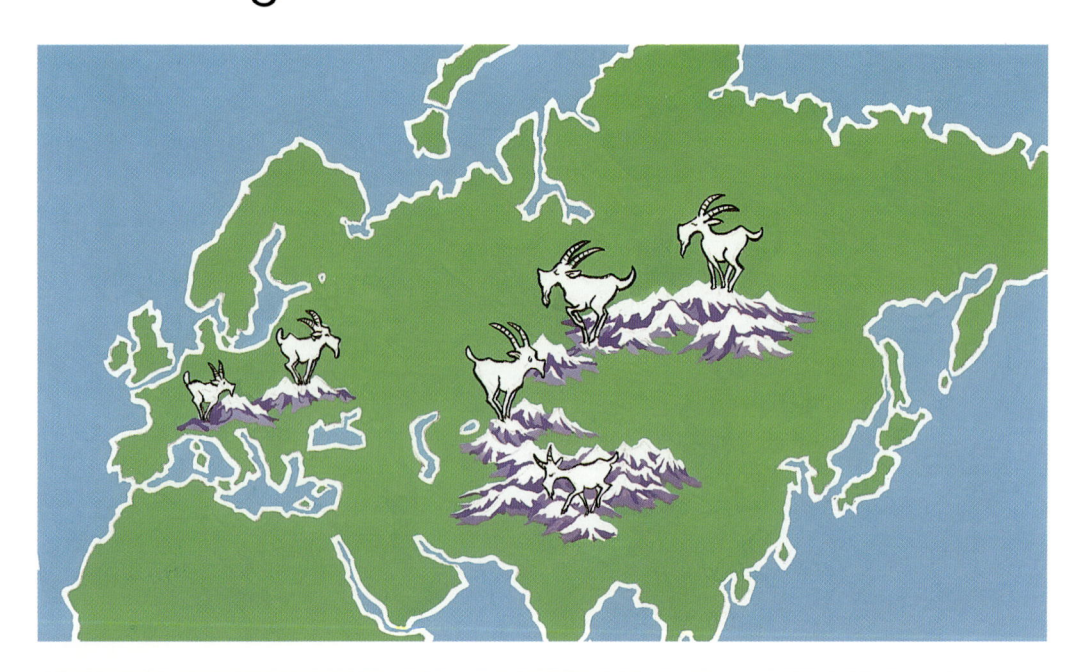

Goats are sometimes tied up to stop them from jumping over fences.

In some countries
herds of goats have eaten
all the young trees,
and all the grass.
Now the land is desert.
Goats can be a pest.

How do goats turn good land into desert?

Goats climb anywhere

Mountain goats are good at climbing. They can jump from rock to rock without falling. Goats can live almost anywhere, and eat almost anything.

Goats eat all the young trees and all the grass.